This book is made up of knots, individual poems and in fact the entire work, poems in push and pull with each other. Thorburn begins with two strands, his maternal Jewish ancestry and his father, a Scots sailor, master of knots. These are not to be solved by the slice of a sword, but are to be traced out into the realm of contemplation. There are many others, returned to throughout the book, whose strengths are the various strands or cords in tension. *Knots* is a book of wonders, to be read and reread again and again. Read it through and then open it anywhere and learn something anew. These are poems to be lived with.
  —Kenneth Fields

These poems take the reader into the heart of the human condition – its disappointments, pain, love and cruelty. Memorable poems about the poet's seaman father, a man of knots, rigging and contradiction, shape the book. Throughout, Thorburn's magnetic and tight poems disclose and loosen the knots—as real as those made of rope—in all of us.
  —Richard Martin

David Thorburn tells us "there is no calculus for the half-life of stories" in poems where "what is lost, what retrieved" can't be and probably shouldn't be added up. "If you marked a coin" and released it to "the oozy waters of finance," Thorburn asks, "would you expect it to return, change from the candyman or grocer?" No, his book says, life doesn't give back change for what we spend it on, just the mystery, the wonder, of transformation. These lyrical poems read like Ovid at eye level: Hecuba and Jackie Gleason; the laugh and grace of eroticism shared by a married couple; Don Quixote and an instruction sheet for the Papco flaring tool. The knots that bind in Thorburn's book are familial, historical, mythic: they embrace and are embraced by something very like a whispered love song.
  —Edward Barrett

KNOTS

DAVID THORBURN

SPUYTEN DUYVIL
New York City

© 2020 David Thorburn
ISBN 978-1-949966-77-0

ACKNOWLEDGMENTS

"June 16, 1953" appeared in *The Threepenny Review* (Winter, 2005)
"The Man I Killed" appeared in *Slate* (March 28, 2006)
"Lise Honorée" appeared with a different title in *The Atlantic Monthly* (Oct. 2007)

Library of Congress Cataloging-in-Publication Data

Names: Thorburn, David, author.
Title: Knots / David Thorburn.
Description: New York City : Spuyten Duyvil, [2020] |
Identifiers: LCCN 2019053662 | ISBN 9781949966770 (paperback)
Subjects: LCGFT: Poetry.
Classification: LCC PS3620.H758 K66 2020 | DDC 811/.6--dc23
LC record available at https://lccn.loc.gov/2019053662

For Barbara

Contents

Dressed for the Day 1

Hat Trick 2

Leaves 3

Nasty Boy 4

Morning Watch 5

Dark Lady 6

June 19, 1953 7

The Man I Killed 8

The Day We Emptied the Old House 9

Near Her 10

Pop Quiz 11

Or Think of Hecuba 12

Running the Break 14

O Jamesy 15

Serious 16

On Deck 18

The Shabbos Milkers 19

Not Always 20

Lise Honorée 23

Slowcount 24

American Story 25

Captain Small at His Ease 26

Rant 27

In Taiwan 28

Cremains 29

Saddam's Face on TV   30

Kransky   31

Poxed   32

Quibble   33

Knots   34

Love Poem   37

In One Story   38

Map It   39

Other Dicks   40

Fort Lauderdale   42

But Still   44

His Happy Head   45

Our Quixote   46

Later   47

Palest Fires May Still Sear   48

Husbandry   49

Crazy Jane   50

The Licenses   52

Defend Me Friends   53

Intelligent Design   54

At Davey's Urn   55

Bridling   56

That Moment   57

Of Supreme Importance   58

Dream Work   59

Dressed For The Day

At 93, in flannel shirt and khakis, he warned me
To make the coffee hot and was a corpse three minutes later.
I touched his arm, raised and dropped it, I touched his forehead,
He seemed asleep but cold. He knew knots and rigging,
Varieties of the hammer, marlinspikes, masonry, copper.

Hat Trick

In "The Adventure of the Blue Carbuncle"
Holmes deduces an intelligent
once respectable

tradesman in degraded lodgings
whose wife no longer
loves him

from a tattered bowler
whose size means brain
power whose broken chin

band proves foresight
corrupted whose yellowing
stains disclose a stumbling

candle-holder sneaking late
to bed in a flat not lit
by gas

unloved by one
so careless of
this grimy unbrushed felt

amazing Dr. Watson
not to mention
us inside

this parallel universe
where crime and married life parse
like this sentence.

Leaves

In the Leopold Museum in Vienna way up,
floors above the sullen Schieles, their grimacing gaudy cunts and faces,
and Janssen's yowling pencils of himself, bug eyes, bloating cheeks, hair
and the top of his head dissolving, irradiating out and away like nebulae,
a winter pastoral so modest you almost pass it by:
hundreds of withered leaves floating in windless air
bring dull color to a regiment of slender trees,
stalks of white bark, branches, the children,
two of them, in winter wrappings small against the trees and empty sky,
foraging for beechnuts in the snow.

Theodor von Hörmann (1840-1895).
Baurenkinder im winterlichen Buchenwald, 1892.
Peasant children in wintry beech forest.
Oil on canvas. Painted in Dachau (Bavaria).

Nasty Boy

Seventy years away from it
am I remembering when
clutching fragments of my front teeth
I ran to Mrs. Green who
used to jab the perfect point of her pencil
into the skulls of bad boys? I wasn't crying
I was mystified, tranced by these broken-off parts of me.

Your teeth were always that way
weren't they said Mrs. Green.
I opened my hand to her. But
these are my teeth. No she said
those are pebbles you've stolen
from the terrarium you nasty boy.

Morning Watch

Tiger loose on deck:
first mate Thorburn

tackles his captain
to stop him firing the hand gun

rips free of his shirt to wave it like a flare
or so he'll tell it years on to his son

as the creature coils in the early glare
and starts her death by water in the fiery air.

Dark Lady

On your throne I see
passing by
the open door.

She laughs.
Here to see your
goddess go?

So pause
and truly see
her sitting there.

Pears and plums are
nothing to this—
breasts belly thighs

flows and valleys:
luscious Europa
on a porcelain throne.

June 19, 1953

Me on my bed reading science fiction
stories from my secret stash,
one about Tibetan monks

who try computers
for their ancient mission,
compiling the nine billion names

of God, my brother Michael
below in the close smoky living room
playing *Für Elise* incessantly

on our clangy upright,
Uncle Aaron at the big table
in our fluorescent kitchen

fiddling with the radio
then calling out to my mother.
They've killed her now. They

had to do it twice. Her skin burned,
it smoked, the second time. Nazis,
mother has to say.

The stars are going out.

The Man I Killed

was in his early 30s, rosaceous,
pocky, the Checker
on a Newark pier. He said

I'll be respected
by New Jersey turds
like you reporters

and these Hoboken wankers
still wearing bog shit.
Don't you get it?

I said No pictures.
Later, off the wharf
the camera guy

used a telephoto lens
as I pointed, for my byline story,
Wildcat Strikers

Shut Port Newark.
The next week they found him
floating near a buoy

dead in Bayonne harbor
in a mess of bootleg whiskey
and my story in the paper.

The Day We Emptied The Old House

we really didn't empty it
we left twenty or thirty books
mostly school and college texts
pamphlets on public health
forty years of *National Geographic*
a wooden chest forever locked by a key lost
at sea between the great wars
according to my father who insisted the chest was worthless
empty and must be left behind
along with his Gravely walking tractor, sickle bar, tiller
and snow plow—given to a young neighbor
whose wife Laurie wept the day we emptied the old house.

Near Her

crouched in homage ready to be petted
knuckles in the ground you look up at her
thinking, almost always to be touching some way
cheek, lips, eyelids against her skin
to be kept near her

Pop Quiz

What the mind retains of old reading
is a problem in narratology now

but such losses and renewals begin
for all of us even before we close a book

and the school teachers who track through Tolstoy
or Dickens every year use their own shortcuts

though as I started to say
there is no calculus for the half-life of stories

what is lost, what retrieved
when one's brain is cued for

the best science fiction story you ever read
Rapunzel, Sherlock Holmes

Don Quixote (not the musical)
Brave Captain Small

Mrs. Elizabeth Darcy
Nabokov, Saint Paul

Demodokus reaching for his lyre
Poldy kissing Molly *there*.

Or Think Of Hecuba

Queen of sufferers Arrowsmith calls her
in his introduction to Euripides' lamentation, miscalled a play.
I am a beast, she cries, I am lower than mud
Abjection is my element, my oxygen
my sons are dead, my husband too
I know I go to exile with all Trojan women
to be used by foreign masters and to die. What worse
is possible or even can be thought?

And yet she's wrong, we learn, for this wailing
takes her early in the play before she truly turns to beast
down on all fours, not human any more, a thing of woe
led down to dark like this by sundry harms
and one especially.
                                   The Herald comes to tell what's worse:
the ritual sacrifice by and for and to the conquering army
of Polyxena her daughter at the tomb of dead Achilles
whose surviving son implores this spirit
to drink *this virgin's fresh blood*
the woman defiant, ripping her robes
exposing her naked breasts,
bare and lovely like a sculptured goddess—
Arrowsmith's Herald relishing his work –
the woman meeting the blade's snick across her throat
with Daddy's Rules of Female Decorum
foremost in her thoughts
at least on this testimony.
                                      The blood
gushed out, and she fell, dying, to the ground,
but even as she dropped, managed to fall somehow
with grace, modestly hiding what should be hidden
from men's eyes.

What dread tangle, what sick flowering is figured and prefigured here!
Pageants of hurt and cankered force spiraling out across two thousand years—
The Perils of Pauline, Game of Thrones, Abu Graib—but also back,
deeper, to a sickened seed, to another daughter's ritual murder
by the king *her father* to his squabbling gods and to his corps
as this first of Western armies gathers on a shore
ready or not to leave their women and belong to war.

Running The Break

Not rushing is the secret, under control, never full-out but in a range of speeds
Keep the ball to the top of the key or else the foul line
Ready to pop from eighteen or bounce-pass left or right
Or take it down the lane and dish or kiss it off the glass yourself or take it to
    the rim or
Kick it to the shooter in the corner.

O Jamesy

It's the *bloat* of modernism I can't abide
the arrogant excessive claim on your time and your brain
the writing makes. You can live your life in *Ulysses*.

Many do. Some of my best friends are Joyceans.
When I first taught at Yale, the eminent Starover Adams
was glad to meet me. Honor the trust your Department

invests in you, he gently said. Your tribe is Jewish, am I right?
When Bloom buys the kidney from his Jewish butcher, none of my students,
not even the Jews, knows Moses Montefiore or what a citron is. My grandfather

Isaac Feller took three of his children with him to Palestine in the 1930s,
leaving his wife and large remaining brood behind on the East Side,
inspired to grow perfect esrogs in the holy land and export them to the States

for Succoth. Grandpa Isaac, the Ralph Kramden of Orthodox entrepreneurs,
went broke at this scheme as at many others, perhaps enticed
by promises of a fruited desert like those Bloom reads thirty years earlier

in the cut sheets at Dlugacz's. My mother in her fervent 20s
had two years among the Zionists and socialists of Jerusalem
and Tel Aviv before returning home to organize American workers,

one of whom, a son of Presbyterian farmers, is said in family lore
to rescue her from danger in a murky sailor's bar and thence to marry her,
beginning the begetting of me, my brothers, this you've read.

If you marked a coin, a quarter or a florin say, with an abrasion
on its face or edge and sent it forth for circulation
on the oozy waters of finance, would you expect it to return,

change from the candyman or grocer?

Serious

Is it like beauty for the old Greeks, in the eye before
it sees, back of the lens, in the capillaries like DNA?

That was when I took my life seriously, Richard said,
remembering standing in line for sixteen hours for a ticket to the Rolling Stones.

He's not serious, says Scholar, meaning
he's readable.

I don't care if you make money, she
said to her son, but you should be a serious

person. Sirius figures in many stories
that are not serious.

This is serious, he thought, when he tasted
her for the first time.

Love is serious, says Nora, but the end
of love is farce.

Almost any task is serious or may be made so
by respect and rigor. Planting tulips. Scouring toilets. Poetry.

Though his workings upon us are terribly serious
the President is not a serious man.

A fever may be serious, weather,
a curriculum.

Great comedy is serious of course. Moliere,
Keaton, Gleason.

One should no more desire
a reward for being serious than

the eye desires praise
for seeing.

On Deck

in icy weather
is one place I see him

pipe burning bowl-down
high boots, hooded slicker

checking lifeboats
securing a hatch

while most of the crew sleeps
and he sips

from a flask of brandy or maybe rum
he carries

in a leather slip-case
that outlasted him.

The Shabbos Milkers

of the Jezreel Valley
drop a floor tile in their buckets

so G-d surveilling inattentively
may see milk spilled,

not drawn by labor
on His sacred day.

My friend Blau derides
this oft-told story

as a fool's invention
since Jews have always seen

animal care as Shabbos duty.
Let's pray he's wrong to put aside so quickly

God as straight man
schlemiel, schmendrick

not fearsome, just a mark,
ready to wink

for His Kibbutzim cows
and dairymen.

Not Always

Not always the civic sailor
or handy geezer
he's less mythological.

There was some secret or lie
way back. He said
or would listen as my mother said

that he had joined the navy lying
about his age
as the first world war was ending

then after written examination
gained Annapolis as one
of only four or ten

enlisted men—
paradise just glimpsed
alas and then . . .

But this is turning
to soap opera or
Conrad where

the unworthy protagonist
sings to please
his father's ghost.

I found a blackjack
among his folded shirts
for use . . . how? against

whom in my safe suburban
house? He owned
a six-shooter in his prime

a double-barreled 12-gauge shotgun
and a scoped 30-30 rifle
he used to kill

a doe in our backyard
in 1952, firing once
from a second story window

to save his garden
from the starving
animal. He did not leave

his firearms to his sons.
A friend I didn't know
took them the day

we emptied the old house.
He brought no killing weapons
when they moved in

maybe afraid my mother
would learn of them
and die

to punish him.
Does that explain
the gentler

weapon
more like a tool
easy to bring

to hand suddenly
asking
strong forearms

iron grip
serious thought to
the bubbled solid

steel tip of it,
not half a golf ball round
good for damage

to the eye
maybe a broken nose
if used quick?

Lise Honorée

Seeing the MGM lion roar
Lise complains she's seen this show before.

My father-in-law's live-in caretaker,
Haitian, *toute douleur,*

She knows Seventh Day Adventist lore
The perfidy of men, how to cure

Oppressive itching. Her
Cooking doesn't please him any more

But he likes her lilting French, her hair
And gentle hands, her living soapy spoor.

Slowcount

She mutters
I'm a martyr
chewing her lip
flushing red as from an immense systolic
surge that threatens to pop her carotid artery
or her squeaky mitral valve

I must calm myself
I don't trust myself to speak to you
says her steady slow counting
half whispered, hoarse with outrage
One two three
trembling as she counts
her thin body electric
crackling
                O she is ready to rise
her anger foaming beneath her
she is levitating, my incandescent mother

American Story

This may be true.
Morris County histories nearly say it.

November 1779.
To escape heavy cares General Washington rides his best gelding

West from his headquarters along wooded
Sloping trails made by the Lenape

Ascending to a modest pinnacle today
Claiming elevation of 1200 feet

Which he names in gratitude for
This sunny day, this fine animal, the smell of piney cold:

Mount Freedom.

Captain Small At His Ease

Deep in his seventies now
and mellowing out

complacent paranoid fuck

won't put his financials
into a computer accessible to
grandchildren

enjoys his dinners though
especially this one
capped off

by a true Havana
from his traveling son

unwrapped carefully o so slow
then savored at the nose
before he smiles and says

"Better than a woman."

Rant

She plans to register at Macy's.
I'm disgusted.

I don't want my friends or Uncle
Michael to buy us gifts

made in sweatshops
in the Philippines.

The plastic
handle of our coffee pot

was made in China I bet
by prisoners.

I could stop our collusion
but then

I'd have to give in
on the priest.

So what.
The shopping engine

kills as many natives
as God these days.

In Taiwan

haloed by flashing yellow lights
along the trafficked narrow two-lane road to Sun Moon Lake

are they kiosks or vitrines?
sunk among gas stations, grocers, commerce in the Buddha

these glass or plastic windows caging
stripped down adolescent girls, ready

in bikinis for their thighs and breasts and
tight young asses

to sell you betel nuts, warm Pepsi,
lucky charms.

Cremains

When she came out to you
it's no excuse that you were ninety
and Claire no longer there to
steer you from your brutal deeps.

Weeping she hears you say you cannot love her
anymore, then that sailor's tale of murdering queers
at night. This isn't the worst to be told of you either.

I wish it could pour out of me—
your stories of square heads, Kallikaks,
Masinos, the saddle cinch used more than once

on me and Andy. But then, your teaching me hand tools,
digging, the constellations. The slingshot
you carved, mythic gift to your David,

perfect organic Y of oak, fitted to my hand,
the work of days, the sling a rigger's boast--
a sculpted tool for killing rabbits and small birds.

At times I want to spit in your ashes,
still in their blue canister, *Cremains
of Frank Thorburn*, shelved
in a back closet where no one goes.

Saddam's Face On TV

Beard and hair untended,
U.S. fingers probing his scalp,

Swabbing inside his mouth.
The enemy's fate: to be flayed

& displayed in cages
Or on stages. See Vice

In the camera's eye, his floating hair,
That darking spot on his old man's temple.

Kransky

for Robert

He was our composite, our projection of ourselves but purer, more clownish. There was a lot of Malamud in him.

Remember how we loved that blasphemous climax when Fidelman *pumping slowly nailed her to his cross.* You used to brag, lording it over me as a married man with constant access, that you'd tested that story's mimesis, cupping Helen's buttocks in your palms as you did the sacred deed.

Something I felt then, how close we were then, has been rare for me and I would honor it here—the way Kransky mesmerized his classes, then, too hasty at the urinal, peed on his shoes beside the Dean.

The way he thought about his teaching, giving strength to his students. The way we made Kransky together in spurts of funny satiric talk and blew off our language exams to play pool and tweak him.

Poxed

He's a green able seaman waiting for a ship
in San Francisco, finding work for food
and rent with a crew that leads
him to a cathedral, up scaffolding to scrape
and paint its gilded ceiling, walking off the job,
the only such desertion of his life, he said,
retching, he said, nauseated
by the poxy Popish air.

Quibble

I see them quibbling over our stuff, loving as they are
At heart. Who gets the kitchen Burra,
Vampirey woman chomping lunch?

Who'll want the brass
Lincoln bookends, poor Abe's right arms
Casualties of our march

To Boston? Which of them will have the Mediterranean
Bedroom, hardly scuffed dear
After 45 years? Your library of architecture,

Our dictionaries? I fear dispersal and dismemberment.

Knots

The *Bride's Necklace* tightens
against resistance
but never fully closes
named and rigged so by an unknown
possibly Scots or Cockney sailor
three hundred years
ago, maybe the Matthew Walker
whose namesake knot's
for sale as a keepsake
from nautical museums in
Sydney and Dunedin.

Among the Lapps and the aborigines of Borneo
knots or knotted garments are taboo
for pregnant women and their husbands lest
the delivery be restricted. No crossing of legs
no locking of house or cupboard until the child comes.

The *Hangman's Noose with Nine Turns* is made exactly
as the *Hangman's Noose with Seven Turns*, except for the two
extra turns, reserved by long tradition for white men.

The *Cuckold's Neck* aka *Half Crown Seizing*
doubles the strength of the *Round Seizing*
by forming the eye at the point where both ropes cross.
This loop knot was invented for the murderous
harpoons they called dolphin strikers
aboard the old whalers.

The secret of the *Turkish Archer Knot*
is lost. Joining slingshot to bowstring,
the knot is illustrated and carefully
described in many documents. But no archer
in a thousand years has achieved
the killing range, eight hundred yards,
of the ancient bowmen who made this knot
sacred to Allah.

The knot in your belly
from bad clams, the one in your chest
for angina. The knot in my head and heart
if you don't come or
when I remember too much.

Othello in his frenzy says the heart
is a cistern where foul toads knot
and gender.

The *Triple Hitch* has saved many lives
including said my father once or twice
a drunken Dutchman lonely for his wife
who pitched headfirst into the forward cargo
hold, and dangled swinging by his hitched right ankle
laughing and vomiting before they cut him down
to hose his mess before the morning watch on
the *SS California*, New York to San Diego
via Havana and the Panama Canal.

The *Knot of Hercules* secures
the girdle barring entrance
to Vestal Virgins' most sacred part,

our oldest knot, the *Square Knot,*
sometimes called the *Reef Knot* nowadays
so strong and perfect to its purposes,

its strength increasing under strain and use,
that it was said to be the god's invention
and was remembered in erotic rites

once widely practiced on patrician wedding nights:
the bridal gown held barely shut by this god's knot
is gently nibbled open by the groom.

Love Poem

She is ruthless and blind
To reason in disputes
Over rights to one's own
Glass of juice, one's salad, one's
Very fork or spoon. Do not leave
Food you want alone with her.

If not complained to, she'll sing
All day & night nonstop except
For meals, nagging, other
Interludes. She requires incessant
Audible distillation of movie subtitles.

Her treatment of cheese is disgraceful.
She tears her favorite, very sharp cheddar, wantonly,
Breaks it in her fingers, never shaves it with a knife, as if
She's famished, as if
She'd never tasted such smooth and salty
Pleasure before.

In One Story

Centuran astronauts sifting debris on a dead planet's
ashen surface unearth
canisters whose gummy contents
are reconstituted after decades of study and lab
work and then projected on devices inferred
from those filmy remnants—generating
archives of conjecture
on these restless violent bipeds, their wheeled projectiles,
spastic mating rituals, the iconography
that always appears at the end:
A Walt Disney Production.

Map It

Map it from its hidden side
See your life that way—
What happens in the kitchen
Not the trades you have in play

What you do in bathrooms
When showering when dry
Not where you work or travel
But where do you get high

What happens in your sleeping rooms
What goes inside your house
Think where you put your nose and tongue
And where you put your mouth.

Other Dicks

The hardboiled gang thinks
hat tricks are stupid
but their adventures

are men's lies too—
even the pebbly fat Continental
Op must fend against

women while godly Bogey
and Marlowe brush away
females as wanton boys

do flies in *Antony
and Cleopatra.*
Worse, they're the enemy

behind the murderer
his source, the ball-cutter
She Who Must Be

Obeyed who dies
at the end of *I the Jury*
doing a strip-tease as

Mike Hammer fires
his thirty-eight straight
into her belly.

Even in Simenon
the women
stink of appetite

and chaos
virgins and proper
grandmothers and one's

brother's spouse
though not Mme. Maigret
mon dieu Brussels sprouts and

Margaux ready
when the great dick climbs the stairs
at eight o'clock

on time as planned
that oozy harem out there
quickening in the dark.

Fort Lauderdale

Ahead of me in the Publix express line
an ancient tiny woman
warrior, newly blonded,
her veiny blue-red face
skeletal, taut,
plastic surgery's revenge—
Nosferatu.

Did I wish you a happy New Year
she asks the young cashier
who says Yes, O Yes
in a Haitian lilt
Thank you, looking away.

The ghosts of mafia dons, B-movie stars
and standup comics of the 1940s and 50s
rumba across the tenth green
at Inverrary on Rock Island Road

where Jackie Gleason played his fabled
clubs, the set complete without an iron,
all woods, even the putter
wondrous made of Irish oak, tungsten,
Corinthian leather
at a price beyond the treasure
of Suleiman or Kubla Khan.

Lawn grass is nasty here
green spiky spears
that prick bare
soles
and say No
to lovers.

The sun's unfriendly fire
peels and pits most outside surfaces
cooks the skin in minutes at midday
sears the unprotected cornea
bleaches, warps or crazes
most things made or breathing.

Beneath this flaking temporary world
lie remnants of the place before
gas stations, malls, this plenitude of Wendys
before air conditioning, before the dredges
back way back
before Major William Lauderdale
aimed his musket at the Seminole
flint blades and arrowheads
debris of teeming mangrove swamp now ossified
dust of conch and beetle wing and turtle shell
dry compost of a million million million
swampy creatures whose surviving emblem
clambers from The Woodlands' golf-course lagoon
most afternoons
to survey his shrunken realm
and bring the sun to his Triassic skin.

But Still

he taught me patience, willingness to stop, back up and start again
when threading metal couplings, to keep these gendered parts clean
    above all, to start a nail

with a sharp exact concussion, one-third strength or less depending on
    conditions—
type of nail, for example, textures being nailed and nailed to—

to know a pick-axe from a mattock, carve a turkey, name some stars,
work the coal furnace, ashes hauled out back to lighten soil for

his Jersey corn, tomatoes, snap peas, rhubarb, cucumber,
strawberries the size of plums.

His Happy Head

Coming to the end now and using it well, sparely, as he should all the time
But never does especially at the start when it seems he's set for months and months

Ounces away from disaster, the misery of facing himself unstoned hidden so deep away
He barely hears it in his happy head, he barely hears it in his happy head, he barely hears it in his happy head.

Our Quixote

Starting out he defies circumstance, then keeps a promise
to Sancho before turning sane to die. His own story

traps him soon enough but first he is great in his purity
and obsession. Though also dangerous —a loon who's

poised with makeshift lance and wobbly horse
to knock your undefended head unsteady. Would he

kill all puppet shows? clear the prisons? What can he teach us,
this relentless old man for whom the world's blood is always allegory

until he's brought home in the cage near the end of Part One, his mess
fouling the straw he sits on, squinting through bars, odorous?

Later

Not till hours later
in the early dark

another leaf-fall bagged and lugged away
is my gratitude sufficient for this afternoon

when I looked up from my raking
as you ascended from your reading chair

then turned facing out, smiling to my eyes
and raised your sweater above your head

to free your sixty-year-old breasts
their fullness, their grave beauty.

Palest Fires May Still Sear

We know of course that for the Jews of Europe
the Messiah did not come

says Mr. Spock on NPR
in his earthly guise as the actor

Nimoy, introducing Lauren Bacall
to read Bernard Guerney's

English version of Isaiah Spiegel's
Yiddish story of the dog Nicky

bereaved by Hitler of his master
Jacob Simon Temkin, fur dealer,

and later exterminated by machine gun with his mistress the widow
Anna Nikolaievna in the Lodz ghetto.

Husbandry

In the stench and black of the animal hold
on the *Adam Mackenzie* out of Liverpool

you speak softly to the Arabian
calming her with Danny Deever and Invictus.

Knowing from your parents' farm
that horses need human voices,

fear confinement, come to harm like children,
you'll feed her carrots, sugar cubes, Tennyson

every day of the voyage, then supervise
her hoisting in rope harness you designed

and rigged to the pier in Brooklyn.
She'll be balky entering the van

until you gentle her and receive your
tip of fifty dollars from the owner.

Crazy Jane

My wife's cousin Jane
dumped a bag
of dogshit

and garbage on her
neighbor's Staten Island
porch because

he refused entrance
to the Roto-Rooter man
sent to snake a clog

flooding sewage
back through toilets
in six houses on his and Jane's

block. She took amphetamines
in senior year and learned
she loved philosophy.

If she'd done this sooner
she thinks she might have stuck
with math

or Nietzsche. Her husband
saw the second tower
fall

and couples holding hands
leap from windows unimaginably
high

so, giving blood
with hundreds
at St. Vincent's

she passes out
from a tourniquet too tight,
wakes

to a halo
of troubled faces
and cries, Oh, no!

I came to help,
not be part
of the problem.

Her first
principle of mothering:
As long as what they're doing

won't make them die,
I'm grateful.

The Licenses

If this were allowed in the Spring rawness of our kind
What may be licensed in the Autumn dry?

The old man's license to drive expires in 2019, though
For years beyond he will remain licentious.

The movie or computer screen gives license
To voyeurs and other voyagers

But we need licenses to build or remodel,
To keep dogs, morphine for the dying, firearms.

To practice law or surgery. Sleep is license
To deeds and trials the waking mind will not remember

Though the body may. The Puritan
Ayatollahs would not license theater

So Henslowe, Shakespeare and their fellows
Played to whores, apprentices and lords

Near the bear-baiting and the Gallows Tree
A space they called The Liberties.

Defend Me, Friends, I Am But Hurt

Admitting Nurse Joan flicks her eyes across mine
as she asks my father, 91, if he's ever been abused
assaulted or physically threatened.   All the time

he answers, all three. By my own body
though, no one else. Then he squints past me
and says, I do the damage in this family.

Intelligent Design

for Adam

The key ingredient of
Chanel No. 5

First made and sold in Paris
In 1921 is

Pau rosa, oil of Amazonia
Rosewood, prolific in Brazil and French Guiana

Twenty years into the last century,
Extinct by 1990.

Wretches hang that jurymen
May dine, and forests die to sweeten

Ear lobes and décolletage
In Moscow and Las Vegas.

At Davey's Urn

Let no one wear a tie.
Let all smoke dope whose mortgages are paid

Or children gone from home or mates content.
No prayers or seminars allowed, no art displayed.

Let's start in twilight on my backyard deck
And drink and eat enough to keep our talk

Alive at least through three or four a.m.
When some may go but most of you stay on

For songs, poached eggs and vivid argument
To keep my drowsy Empress awake

And save the earth from ill and fix the sky.
O wait till dawn before you say goodbye.

BRIDLING

At the insinuation
He's shit to his master,
The bridler toys with revenge

Maybe bridling My Lord's
Big chestnut
With a virgin bit

She'll spit in rage
In half a mile
And rub His Fucking Arsehole

Off her back against
The willow branches
In the swamp along the river.

How many boys and men
In saddlery or
Harness-making then?

He's not primitive, technology-deprived,
But literate, generous, adept among
His world's deep systems of transport,

Caste and commerce. He won't bloody
The grand creature's tender
Mouth *lucky for Poxnose*

And selects a gentler
Harness, hating how she
Lifts her quivering lips
To take the iron in.

That Moment

in Conrad when Jim
knows he's dead:
the skin of the hull against his palm

trembling to dissolve or
spume all away
in the boiling ocean.

Or when the magazine exploded
and you lay bobbing near
those corpses and one other survivor

who joined the madhouse for
life after his body got well
in that veterans' hospital

you say healed you O my worthy father
from three days floating among the dead
bleeding from the left side of your head

ear hemorrhaging, face into the
cooling gory liquid, out again to breathe
sleep as poisoned and as yearned for as the water.

Of Supreme Importance

—for Arthur Mattuck

The instruction sheet for the Papco Flaring Tool
fits in your palm when folded and opens
to three inches by four and a half,
both sides densely printed.
It's protected in a plastic sleeve that's yellow now
and hard enough to cut your finger tips.
Two machinist's drawings and 304 words
name its parts—including Body, Lever, Strap,
Strap Bushing, Eccentric Adjusting Screw,
Clamp Yoke, Indexing Ball, Cone Dowel Pin—
and explain the working of this plumber's hand-tool,
how the compression screw and swivel cone swing aside for clear
sighting, the hexagon clamp expanding or contracting
on calibrated gears that turn precisely after seventy years.
Papco Forge and Foundry, Dayton, Ohio,
machined the instrument between the two World Wars
and produced this tiny illustrated bible
which lauds one virtue of the tool,
its ability to close-flare very short lengths of copper,
as "of supreme importance to refrigeration men."

Dream Work

Car repair was not in his repertoire but here
he is, working a ratchet wrench
under the hood of my blue station wagon
the 68 Ford with a hot spot in the cargo space where
the kids would dry their bathing suits
after the beach.

He turns from the work now, hobbling strangely.
My shoes, he says, where
are my shoes?

The kids are grown and far away, the shoes
are ten years gone to Goodwill with his decent shirts
and the woolen longjohns he wore at sea
before he came ashore
to make me.

DAVID THORBURN has been a teacher of literature for 55 years. He was born in Manhattan and grew up in an old farmhouse in Randolph, New Jersey before it became a suburb. He's written a book on Joseph Conrad and many essays and reviews on literature and media. *Knots* is his first book of poetry.

Cover design: Barbara Thorburn

www.ingramcontent.com/pod-product-compliance
Lightning Source LLC
Chambersburg PA
CBHW030200100526
44592CB00009B/379